HOW TO DRAW KNIGHTS AND CASTLES

Mark Bergin

PowerKiDS press™

New York

Published in 2012 by The Rosen Publishing Group, Inc.
29 East 21st Street, New York, NY 10010

Editor: Rob Walker
U.S. Editor: Kara Murray

Library of Congress Cataloging-in-Publication Data

Bergin, Mark.
  How to draw knights and castles / by Mark Bergin. — 1st ed.
      p. cm. — (How to draw)
  Includes index.
  ISBN 978-1-4488-4514-9 (library binding) — ISBN 978-1-4488-4522-4 (pbk.) —
  ISBN 978-1-4488-4530-9 (6-pack)
  1. Knights and knighthood in art—Juvenile literature.
  2. Castles in art—Juvenile literature.
  3. Drawing—Technique—Juvenile literature.
  I. Title. II. Series.
  NC825.K54B47 2012
  741.2—dc22

                    2010051197

Manufactured in Heshan, China

CPSIA Compliance Information: Batch #SS1102PK: For Further Information contact
Rosen Publishing, New York, New York at 1-800-237-9932

PAPER FROM
SUSTAINABLE
FORESTS

Contents

Making a Start

Learning to draw is about looking and seeing. Keep practicing and get to know your subject. Use a sketchbook to make quick drawings. Start by doodling and experimenting with shapes and patterns. There are many ways to draw but this book shows only some methods. Visit art galleries, look at artists' drawings, and see how your friends draw. Above all, though, find your own way.

Practice sketching people in everyday surroundings. This will help you draw faster and train you to capture the main elements of a pose.

Remember that practice makes perfect. If a drawing looks wrong, start again. Keep working at it. The more you draw, the more you will learn.

Perspective

If you look at any object from different viewpoints, you will see that whichever part is closest to you looks larger, and the part farthest away from you looks smallest. Drawing in perspective is a way of creating a feeling of depth, or of suggesting three dimensions on a flat surface.

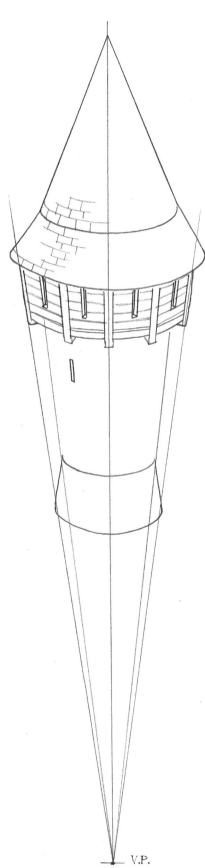

V.P.

V.P. = vanishing point

Low eye level
(view from below)

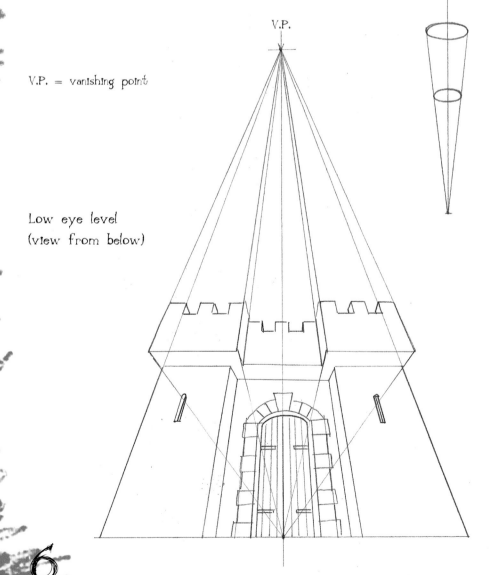

— V.P.

Two-point perspective uses two vanishing points: one for lines running along the length of the object, and one on the opposite side for lines running across the width of the object.

Two-point perspective drawing

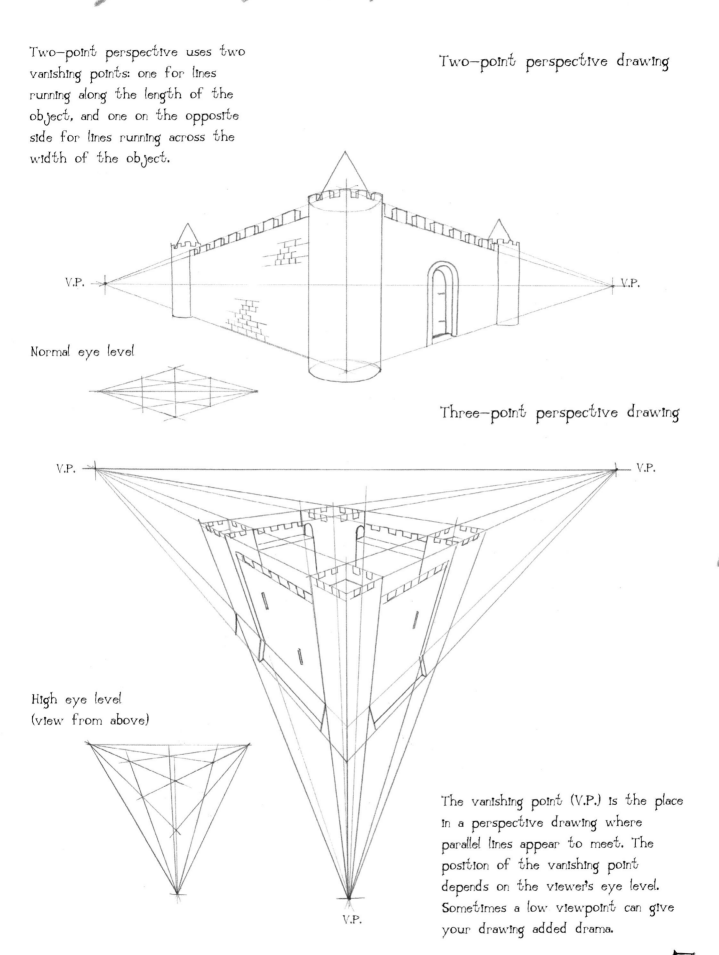

V.P.

V.P.

Normal eye level

Three-point perspective drawing

V.P.

V.P.

High eye level
(view from above)

The vanishing point (V.P.) is the place in a perspective drawing where parallel lines appear to meet. The position of the vanishing point depends on the viewer's eye level. Sometimes a low viewpoint can give your drawing added drama.

V.P.

7

Drawing Materials

Try using different types of drawing papers and materials. Experiment with charcoal, wax crayons, and pastels. All pens, from felt-tips to ballpoints, will make interesting marks. Try drawing with pen and ink on wet paper for a variety of results.

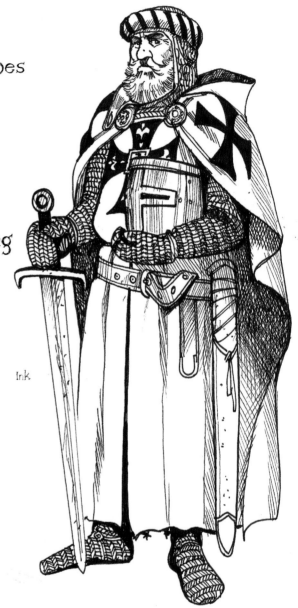

Ink

Hard **pencil** leads are grayer and soft pencil leads are blacker. Hard pencils are graded from #2½ to #4 (the hardest). A #1 pencil is a soft pencil, and a #2 is medium.

Pencil

Lines drawn in ink cannot be erased, so keep your ink drawings sketchy and less rigid. Don't worry about mistakes as these lines can be lost in the drawing as it develops.

Charcoal is very soft and can be used for big, bold drawings. Ask an adult to spray your charcoal drawings with fixative to prevent smudging.

Felt—tip

Pastels are even softer than charcoal and come in a wide range of colors. Ask an adult to spray your pastel drawings with fixative to prevent smudging.

You can create special effects in a drawing done with **wax crayons** by scraping parts of the color away.

Silhouette is a style of drawing that uses only a solid black shape.

Ink silhouette

Studies from Life

Drawing from life or photographs can help you identify shape and form. It can also develop both your drawing skills and your eye for detail.

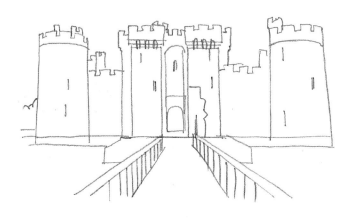

Make a tracing of a photograph and draw a grid of squares on it.

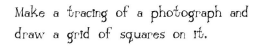

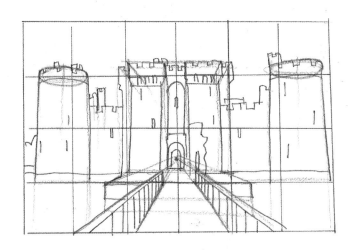

Now take a piece of drawing paper of the same proportion and draw a grid on it, either enlarging or reducing the scale of the square's size, You can now copy shapes from each square of the tracing to the drawing paper, using the grid to guide you.

A quick sketch can often be as informative as a careful drawing that has taken many hours.

To make your drawing look three-dimensional, decide which side the light source is coming from, and put in areas of shadow where the light doesn't reach.

Sketch in an overall tone and add surrounding textures to create interest and a sense of movement. Pay attention to the position of your drawing on the paper. This is called composition.

Castle Keep and Towers

The keep is the central, or core, castle building. Towers were built at intervals along the castle walls to strengthen them and provide accommodation for castle workers or visitors.

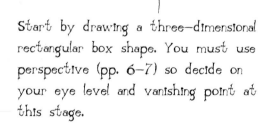

Start by drawing a three-dimensional rectangular box shape. You must use perspective (pp. 6–7) so decide on your eye level and vanishing point at this stage.

Add a tower at each corner of the keep.

You can use a ruler to make sure the initial construction lines are straight. Freehand drawing will look more interesting after that.

Sketch in doorways.

Draw in battlements or crenellations to the top of the castle walls and towers.

Mark in the position of the windows.

Work your way around the battlements to give them a three-dimensional effect at the top.

Draw the tiled roofs.

Draw the stairway and door.

Carefully draw the brickwork to make the stone look more realistic.

Add details to the stonework over all doors and windows.

Add more detail to the base of the keep walls.

Draw the stairs and railing.

13

Gatehouse and Drawbridge

A drawbridge is usually over a moat or ditch and can be raised or lowered. At the first sign of danger, the drawbridge would be raised, making it impossible for an enemy to cross into the castle.

Start by drawing a three-dimensional rectangular box shape using a vanishing point.

Give the gatehouse added drama by using a low eye-level viewpoint.

Extend this section to make the upper section of the gatehouse larger.

Use curved lines to draw the rounded sections of the gatehouse.

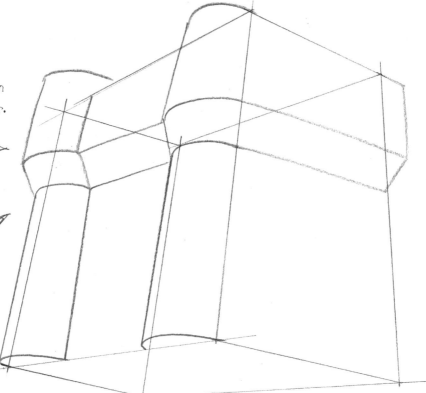

Add more detail.

Sketch in the battlements along the top of the walls.

Draw the position of the door and windows.

Draw the three-dimensional detail.

Softly draw lines to create brickwork.

Complete the battlements by making them three-dimensional.

Draw in wall and corner tower.

Finish by drawing the moat and adding a wooden drawbridge.

Add detail to the door and archway.

15

How Castles Developed

A castle is a fortress built for defense against enemy armies. It was also the home of a lord and his followers. People who lived on the castle lands were protected, too.

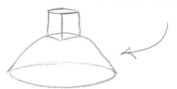

Early castles consisted of a wooden tower built on an artificial mound, or motte.

A strong wooden fence runs around the tower.

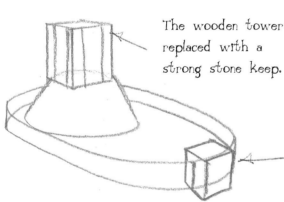

The wooden tower is replaced with a strong stone keep.

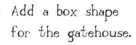

Add a box shape for the gatehouse.

The fenced enclosure is called a bailey.

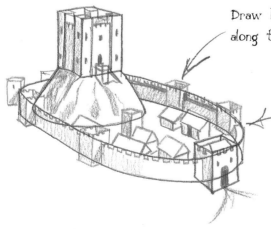

Draw box-shaped stone towers spaced along the curtain wall.

The outbuildings include a chapel and space for livestock.

Add details to the castle, gatehouse, and battlements.

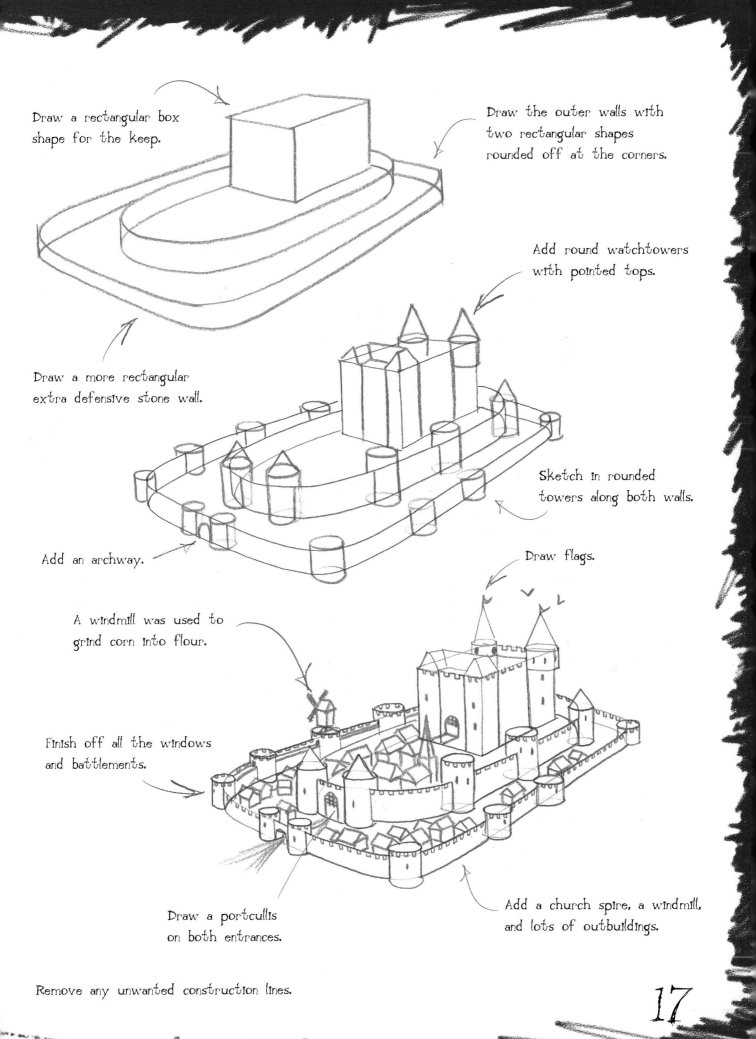

Draw a rectangular box shape for the keep.

Draw the outer walls with two rectangular shapes rounded off at the corners.

Add round watchtowers with pointed tops.

Draw a more rectangular extra defensive stone wall.

Sketch in rounded towers along both walls.

Add an archway.

Draw flags.

A windmill was used to grind corn into flour.

Finish off all the windows and battlements.

Draw a portcullis on both entrances.

Add a church spire, a windmill, and lots of outbuildings.

Remove any unwanted construction lines.

Castle Detail

Skilled archers could fire up to 10 arrows a minute. A well-aimed arrow could kill a man about 300 feet (100 m) away.

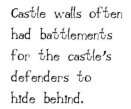

Castle walls often had battlements for the castle's defenders to hide behind.

These holes in the floor were called murder holes.

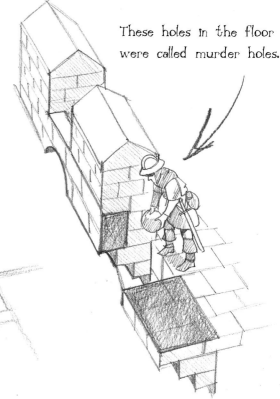

Horizontal and vertical lines give the effect of stone brickwork.

Use construction lines to help make the battlements look three-dimensional.

Use construction lines to help you experiment with proportion.

"Arrow loops" were often wider on the inside to give the archer a wider field of vision.

Arrow loops are the slits in the walls through which archers could fire arrows. These slits can be different shapes.

Bolts and handles can make a door look older and more realistic.

Try marking a center point to help draw hard shapes.

Knights Through the Ages

Knights were not ordinary soldiers. They were the elite fighting men of their time. They traveled on horseback, wore high-quality armor, and used swords and lances.

Draw a simple stick figure.

Design your own shield markings.

Knights wore chainmail underneath their armor.

Sketch in nicks and dents on the shield to make it look more battle worn.

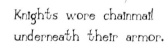

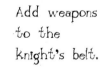

Add weapons to the knight's belt.

Shields and helmets came in different shapes and sizes.

Draw simple stick figures to try out different stances or poses before you begin to draw.

Some helmets had visors to cover the knight's face.

The shield markings identified each knight.

Knights wore armored gloves called gauntlets.

Add shading to areas where light would not reach.

Add spurs.

Add detail and shading to the metal armor. Leave some areas of the armor white as highlights on the metal surface.

Draw a belt and chainmail skirt called jupon.

Remove any unwanted construction lines.

21

Knight

Knights were expected to be honorable and brave and to protect the weak. This code of conduct became known as chivalry.

Head

Draw a vertical line through the center.

Main body

Draw in ovals for the head, neck, body, and hips.

Hips

Center line

Draw the helmet.

Add circles for the hands.

Light and Shade

The shading in a drawing depends on the strength and direction of the light source. See how the shading is darker for all those parts of the knight's body farthest from the light source.

Draw simple shapes for the feet.

Sketch in tube shapes for the arms and legs.

Use long, sweeping lines for the knight's tunic.

Add more detail to the helmet.

Draw the sword with the
hand clenched around it.

Draw the shield
and strap.

Add vertical shading to
the helmet to give the
impression of metallic shine.

Sketch in the belt
and scabbard.

Shade the sword.

Add chips and
dents to the shield.

Draw the fabric turned
back to create interest.

Draw a scalelike pattern
for the chainmail.

Add a coat of arms
design to the shield
and tunic.

Add the knee
guards and spurs.

Add shading to the fabric
to create soft folds.

Remove any unwanted construction lines.

23

Knight on the Attack

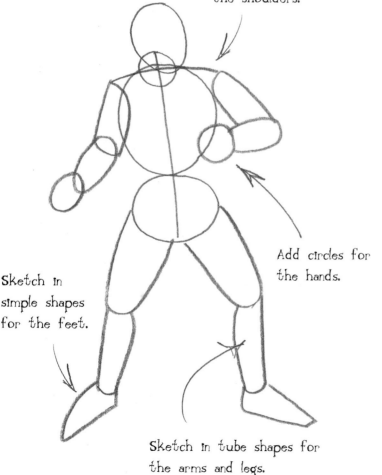

In times of war, a king would call up his knights and lords to fight. Battles were won by the knights and archers fighting together with a planned course of attack.

Draw three ovals for the head, neck, hips, and main body.

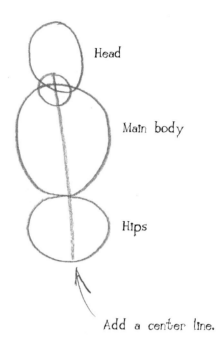

Head

Main body

Hips

Add a center line.

Draw a line to indicate the shoulders.

Add circles for the hands.

Sketch in simple shapes for the feet.

Sketch in tube shapes for the arms and legs.

Action Poses

Try drawing basic stick figures to help you decide on a character's pose and how he might move.

Add a cone-shaped helmet and position the eyes, nose, and mouth.

Draw a curved line around the face and across the chest for the chainmail hood.

Add a sword.

Sketch in the shield and strap.

Add a belt.

Draw the gauntlets.

Draw detail on the knight's armor, such as knee guards called poleyns.

Add the knight's foot guards called sabatons.

Finish drawing the face and helmet details.

Add a design to the knight's shield and tunic.

Shade in the sword.

Finish off all details on the knight's armor, belt, and tunic.

Shade the areas where light would not reach.

Add shade to the armor so it looks like metal.

Remove any unwanted construction lines.

Jousting Knight

In a joust, knights fought on a one-to-one basis. The knights charged at each other at great speed and tried to knock each other off their horses.

Draw in basic shapes for the knight's head, body, and hips.

Add a curved line from the head, down the neck, and across the back.

Knight body

Head

Front

Hind quarters

Add a line for the knight's leg.

Draw a circular shape for the head and two larger ones for the body.

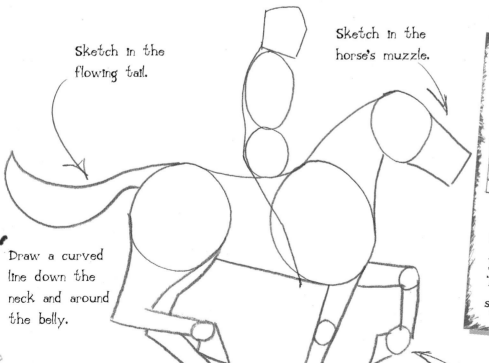

Sketch in the flowing tail.

Sketch in the horse's muzzle.

Draw a curved line down the neck and around the belly.

Draw the horse's legs and hooves. Add circles to indicate the joints.

Using a Mirror
Use a mirror to check out your drawing in reverse. This is a good way to spot mistakes.

Sketch in the decorative fabric on the helmet.

Use straight lines to draw the lance.

Add a saddle and belt under the horse's belly.

Sketch in the horse's eyes, ears, mouth, and nostrils. Indicate the horse's hood.

Add reins and a stirrup.

Sketch in simple shapes for the knight's armor.

Use curved, flowing lines for the skirt of the horse's caparison, or surcoat.

Add a crest and complete the detail on the helmet.

Add the shield.

Use curved, flowing lines for the horse's tail.

Add a dagger, shoulder guards, and a belt.

Draw a coat of arms design on the horse's surcoat.

Add tufts to the hooves.

Shade the areas where light would not reach.

Draw a suggestion of the ground.

27

A Traveling Knight

Knights setting off to fight in enemy territory had to take all kinds of supplies with them, including clothes, food, weapons, armor, tents, bedding, medicines, spare horses, and axes to cut firewood.

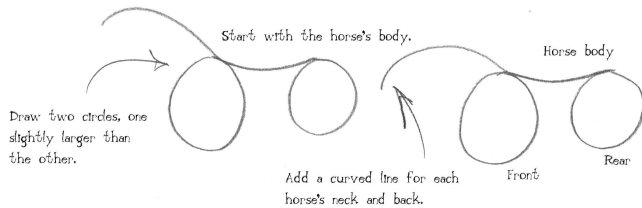

Start with the horse's body.

Draw two circles, one slightly larger than the other.

Add a curved line for each horse's neck and back.

Horse body

Front

Rear

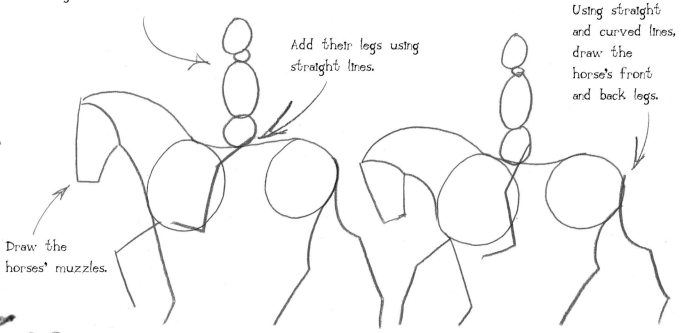

Draw simple shapes for the head, neck, body, and hips of the knight and his steward.

Add their legs using straight lines.

Using straight and curved lines, draw the horse's front and back legs.

Draw the horses' muzzles.

Sketch in the saddle and hand clutching a spear.

Add the knight's features, a helmet, armor, and a shield.

Add the steward's features, headdress, and clothing.

Draw rounded shapes to indicate baggage.

Draw both horses' eyes and ears.

Add the reins, bridles, and horses' manes.

Add the horses' tails.

Draw in each horse's belly.

Draw in the horse's hooded surcoat and reins.

Sketch in both horses' legs and hooves.

Add detail to the knight's armor.

Finish off the spear and add a flag.

Complete the steward's clothing.

Draw the same coat of arms on the shield and the horse's surcoat.

Shade the horses.

Add stirrups.

Shade in areas where the light doesn't reach.

29

Knights in Battle

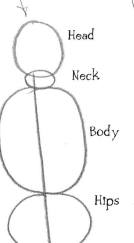

Knights fought with swords, lances, maces, and battle–axes. This action pose shows two knights in battle, slashing at each other with their swords. It was important for them to keep their sword blades very sharp.

Draw both figures using ovals for the head, neck, body, and hips.

Head

Neck

Body

Hips

Add a vertical line to indicate the position of the body.

To show the right arm bent at the elbow, draw one oval smaller than the other and slightly overlapping,

Add the arms and legs using simple tube shapes.

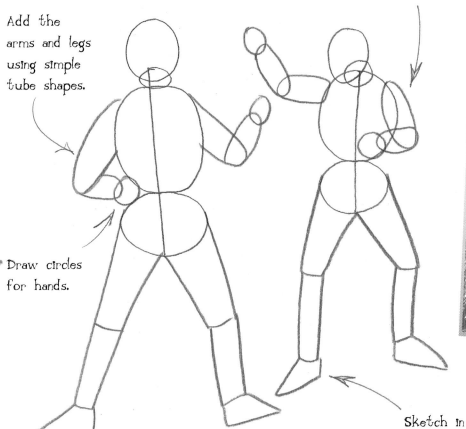

Draw circles for hands.

Composition

Framing your drawing in a square or a rectangle can make it look completely different.

Sketch in simple shapes for the feet.

Sketch in fold lines on the knight's back to indicate movement.

Draw the swords.

Sketch in the eyes, nose, and mouth.

Sketch different-shaped helmets.

Draw two shields.

Draw the tunics.

Add scabbards.

Add shading to the helmets to make them look like metal.

Add shield markings and nicked edges to create a battle-worn look.

Draw a scaly pattern for the knight's chainmail.

Draw the construction of the back view of this shield.

Add a battleground setting with fallen helmets, shields, and fired arrows.

Add shadows to make the knights look three-dimensional.

31

Glossary

center line (SEN–tur LYN) Often used as the starting point of the drawing, it marks the middle of the object or figure.

composition (kom–puh–ZIH–shun) The arrangement of the parts of a picture on the drawing paper.

construction lines (kun–STRUK–shun LYNZ) Guidelines used in the early stages of a drawing and usually erased later.

fixative (FIK–suh–tiv) A type of resin used to spray over a finished drawing to prevent smudging. It should be used only by an adult.

light source (LYT SORS) The direction from which the light seems to come in a drawing.

perspective (per–SPEK–tiv) A method of drawing in which near objects are shown larger than faraway objects to give an impression of depth.

pose (POHZ) The position assumed by a figure.

proportion (pruh–POR–shun) The correct relationship of scale between each part of the drawing.

vanishing point (VA–nish–ing POYNT) The place in a perspective drawing where parallel lines appear to meet.

Index

Web Sites

Due to the changing nature of Internet links, PowerKids Press has developed an online list of Web sites related to the subject of this book. This site is updated regularly. Please use this link to access the list:

32 www.powerkidslinks.com/htd/knights/